D0119941

be   ~~

20th CENTURY ISSUES

CENSORSHIP
Changing Attitudes 1900-2000

Scarlett MccGwire

WAYLAND

TWENTIETH CENTURY ISSUES SERIES

Censorship
Crime and Punishment
Medical Ethics
Poverty
Racism
Women's Rights

Produced for Wayland Publishers Limited by Discovery Books Limited, Unit 3, 37 Watling Street, Leintwardine, Shropshire SY7 0LW, England

Editor: Patience Coster
Series editor: Alex Woolf
Series design: Mind's Eye Design, Lewes
Consultant: Regina Jere-Malanda

First published in 1999 by Wayland Publishers Limited, 61 Western Road, Hove, East Sussex BN3 1JD, England

Find Wayland on the internet at http://www.wayland.co.uk

British Library Cataloguing in Publication Data
MccGwire, Scarlett
Censorship: changing attitudes 1900-2000. - (Twentieth century issues)
1. Censorship - History - 20th century - Juvenile literature
I. Title
363.3'1'0904

ISBN 0-7502-2465-7

Printed and bound in Italy by G. Canale & C.S.p.A., Turin

Picture acknowledgements
Corbis 7 (Owen Franken), 25 (Tim Page), 27 (David Turnley), 52, 55 (Leif Skoogfors), 57 (Robert Maass), 58 (Kevin Fleming); Corbis-Bettmann 4, 26, 28; Corbis-Bettmann/Reuter 43; Corbis/Bettman/UPI 16, 30, 37; Mary Evans Picture Library 9; Historical Picture Archive/Corbis 12; Hulton-Deutsch Collection/Corbis 13, 29; Hulton Getty 6, 8, 38, 42 (Steve Eason), 50; Hulton Getty/Nordik Pressfoto 15; Impact 14 (Mark Henley), 18 (Piers Cavendish), 44 (Gideon Mendel), 48 (John Arthur); Library of Congress/Corbis 10; Popperfoto 45, 49 (Isabelle Simon), 53; Popperfoto/Reuter 21 (Yannis Behrakis), 41 (Sergei Karpukhin), 47; Rex Features 17; Topham Picturepoint 19, 20, 32, 33, 36, 39, 46, 51; UPI/ Corbis-Bettmann 34; Wayland Picture Library 5, 23, 40, 59.

Cover: main picture shows Tibetan exiles staging a silent protest against Chinese rule in their country (Popperfoto/Reuter); black-and-white pictures show, top to bottom, Stalin and Lenin editing the newspaper, Pravda (Topham Picturepoint); Nazi youths burning books at Salzburg in 1938 (Topham Picturepoint); and a photographer being stopped by police in Berlin (Rex Features).

CONTENTS

WHAT IS CENSORSHIP?

OPINION

'Give me the liberty to know, to utter, and to argue freely according to conscience, above all liberties.'
John Milton, *Areopagitica*, 1644.

OPINION

'Free speech is about as good a cause as the world has ever known. But, like the poor, it is always with us and gets shoved aside in favour of things which seem at some given moment more vital.... Everybody favours free speech in the slack moments when no axes are being ground.'
Heywood Broun, American commentator, 1926.

Censorship is the act of suppressing publications, films, television programs, plays, letters and so on which are considered to be obscene, blasphemous or politically unacceptable. A person authorized to carry out this activity is called a censor. The term censor is also used to describe a person who controls or suppresses the behaviour of others, usually on moral grounds. Censorship takes many forms: books may be banned or cut, newspapers may have articles withdrawn, plays are not given licences and therefore cannot be performed. In some countries, where people are persecuted for their religious or political beliefs, they are often subject to censorship and banned from speaking in public or publishing their writings.

Throughout history, people in positions of power – government officials, private individuals, religious

Down the ages, religious leaders have banned books they deem to be offensive. Here clergymen titter as they burn condemned books.

leaders – have consistently sought to suppress materials they deem to be unacceptable. When Gutenberg invented the printing press in the mid-fifteenth century, the Pope in Rome issued a list of books he believed should be banned. When movies became popular during the early years of the twentieth century, studio executives in Hollywood realized that the industry would have to censor itself, or else the government would.

Sometimes the act of censoring is hard to detect, at other times, it is obvious. In many countries the government owns or has control of nearly all forms of media. In 1949 China became a Communist country under Mao Zedong. Dissidents (people who disagreed with government policy) were forced to recant their ideas in public in order to discredit them.

In 1633, the astronomer Galileo was imprisoned for saying that the Earth was not the centre of the universe. He was released only when he recanted his idea.

In 1977 Donald Woods, the editor of the Daily Dispatch *in South Africa, was banned. Here he reads about the government's action against him in the first issue of the newspaper he was prohibited from editing.*

A further example of obvious political censorship took place in South Africa. For most of the twentieth century South Africa was ruled by a white government, even though the majority of the population was black. For much of this time the white government operated a system called apartheid (apartness), in which black people were considered to be second-class citizens and were not given the same rights as whites. Under a law passed in 1950, the government had wide-ranging powers to 'ban' people who expressed views opposed to apartheid. Under the banning order, the victim could not be quoted in any way. Writers who disagreed with the government's racist policies would not find a publisher within South Africa.

However, despite various examples of government control, the most prevalent form of censorship today is self-censorship. As a rule, people know what is and what is not acceptable, and make efforts not to overstep the mark. There is also a consensus in society that some displays of violence and sex, publication of personal attacks, certain information about government policies and so on should be withheld from the general public. So, if some censorship is acceptable in a democratic society, the main question is: where should the line be drawn, and by whom?

Censorship is always justified by the censors, who argue that it is in the interests of national security, or to protect children, or to save people from depravity. Most of us would agree that in times of war a country must keep secrets from the enemy. But should newspaper editors be fed lies to print, as they were by governments during the Second World War? And is a high level of government secrecy necessary in peace time? Books, magazines, films and television programs are censored 'to protect the public', but who has the right to judge what will deprave and corrupt? Some books that we now consider to be fine literature have at some time faced the censor's wrath.

> **OPINION**
>
> 'God forbid that any book should be banned. The practice is as indefensible as infanticide.'
> Dame Rebecca West, British author, 1928.

Neo-Nazis, like this young German man, express racist views that many people find offensive. But does society have the right to censor their acts of free expression?

This book looks at the arguments that have been posed for and against censorship throughout the twentieth century. Censorship reflects the society in which it operates, not just the level of political freedom within that society but its attitudes towards sex and religion too. However, although the ways in which the censors wield their power

have changed, the arguments about what should be censored, and why, remain basically the same.

THE VICTORIAN LEGACY

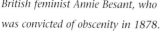

British feminist Annie Besant, who was convicted of obscenity in 1878.

The dawning of the twentieth century marked the end of the Victorian era. However, the prudery and censorship associated with the late nineteenth century persisted even after the death of Britain's longest reigning monarch in 1901. At that time the world was dominated by a handful of European powers. Britain, France, Spain, Portugal, the Netherlands, Italy and Germany governed colonies which made up most of Africa and a large part of Asia. The influence of these colonial powers was considerable.

During the nineteenth century many members of the middle class had concentrated on moral campaigns against vice. Groups like the National Vigilance Association in Britain were well established by the end of the 1880s. They mounted prosecutions against people who conspired to 'corrupt'. Although the government distanced itself from these groups, they were successful in influencing public opinion and setting standards.

THE SPREAD OF LITERACY

Until 1850, newspapers were heavily taxed in Britain. This prevented poorer people reading them and deterred impoverished radicals from starting up their own publications. The government announced that 'persons exercising the power of the press should be men of some respectability and property'. But the education of the working class was also a feature of nineteenth-century life. In Britain, school attendance became compulsory in 1880. Books

How the French cartoonist Grandeville depicted the censor in 1840.

and newspapers were published to appeal to a popular mass market. For the first time, working people could read what they chose. This enlightenment of 'the dark masses' alarmed many members of the ruling class (the upper and middle classes), who feared that the influence of radical writers would cause the people to revolt or riot.

In 1880, the European press was mostly made up of papers dealing in serious news, aimed at the upper and middle classes. At this time in Europe, the vote was being extended from men who owned property to all men. (Women were not allowed to vote until much later.) The invention of the modern rotary press, first used in London by *The Times* in 1886, dramatically increased the speed with which news was disseminated. And the widespread use of the wireless telegraph and the newly invented telephone made it possible to transmit information across the world in an instant. The twentieth century was destined to be a century of mass communication.

> **OPINION**
>
> 'It is by the goodness of God that in our country we have those three unspeakably precious things: freedom of speech, freedom of conscience, and the prudence never to practise either of them.'
> Mark Twain, American writer, 1897.

A group of newsboys in New York in 1910. Technological progress meant that papers were printed in large numbers. They were designed with catchy headlines and stories to appeal to a mass market.

As the circulation figures of many newspapers topped a million or more, the European and North American governments became increasingly worried about people they suspected of attempting to undermine their authority.

In Germany, during the first six months of 1913, over one hundred socialist journalists were convicted of breaking censorship laws and many of them were jailed. In the USA, thirty states introduced statutes prohibiting the dissemination of obscene materials. Meanwhile Britain was regarded as a beacon of political freedom – a land which set a democratic example for virtually all other countries, especially with regard to censorship and civil liberties.

In Europe and North America, the Establishment (those people who controlled the government, civil service, armed forces and the Church) was worried about the growth of a subversive culture. By blending political, social and sexual deviances, this culture was thought to threaten the very fabric of society.

Certainly a glance at what was happening in India confirmed the Establishment's worst fears. During the nineteenth century, the 'vernacular', or Indian languages press, had been severely censored by the British authorities because of violent attacks made on the government and British rule. After censorship was lifted towards the end of the century, the Indian nationalist movement used the free press to advance its cause, eventually winning independence for India in 1947.

CENSORSHIP IN THE ARTS

As urban populations grew, the size of audiences hungry for entertainment also increased. While books and newspapers introduced a new readership to new ideas, the theatre and, later, the cinema introduced new ideas to a mass audience gathered together in one place. Establishment fears of the dangers of a mass audience resulted in strict measures to curb freedom of expression in the arts. In Britain, at the turn of the century, all plays had to be cleared by the Lord Chamberlain's Office before they could be performed. Most political plays were banned. In 1907, the Gilbert and Sullivan operetta, *The Mikado*, was stopped because it was thought that it might offend a visiting Japanese prince (although, ironically, the Japanese bands on the warship that brought him to Britain were playing songs from the operetta). Religious plays were difficult to get past the censors. Even conformist interpretations of biblical stories were closely scrutinized. After many years, *Samson and Delilah* finally managed to gain a licence. But there was a ban on any criticism of religious orthodoxy.

> **OPINION**
>
> 'I have studied Ibsen's plays carefully, and all the characters... appear to be morally deranged.'
> Mr Pigott, a censor appointed by the British government, speaking in 1892.

> **OPINION**
>
> 'Censorship has always been one of the reasons I have not ventured into play-writing.'
> H G Wells' evidence to the 1909 Enquiry into Censorship which was set up by the British government.

OPINION

In 1916 the British Home Secretary's Report from Police Chiefs declared: 'the recent increase in juvenile delinquency is, to a considerable extent, due to demoralizing cinematograph films.'

A French poster for the play, La Dame aux Camellias. *The play was banned in Britain because it depicted the life of a courtesan.*

In the main, however, the censor's sights were fixed on sex. Producers soon devised ways of getting round the system. It appeared to be the case that the more frivolous the play, the more the producer could get away with. Any form of music was considered to be frivolous. So the play *La Dame aux Camellias*, about a courtesan and her lover, was banned in England, while the opera *La Traviata* (a musical version of the same play) was not. The play *Mumma Vanna* was banned for possibly inciting lewd thoughts. It was the story of a woman who, in order to save the inhabitants of her town from war, had to go to the opposing commander nude under her cloak. The audience never saw beneath the cloak and she was allowed to return to her people untouched, but the thought of a naked woman under a cloak was too much for the censor. Some commentators of the day pointed out that we are all naked underneath our clothes.

The censors also reacted to pressure from the public. In 1907, Richard Strauss's opera *Salome* was denounced as immoral by New York audiences. It was withdrawn from performance at the Metropolitan Opera House after only a few days. The offending scene contained a dance in which Salome took off seven veils.

Fears of the new and the challenging have always contributed to calls for censorship. In Berlin, the German Empress Auguste Victoria personally intervened to prevent the staging of Richard Strauss's innovative opera *Der Rosenkavalier*. In New York, George Bernard Shaw's play, *Mrs Warren's Profession*, was closed by the police for immorality because it dealt openly with the issue of prostitution. Critics denounced it as 'revolting in theme' and 'a pervading poison'.

As the twentieth century progressed, more and more people flocked to movie theatres to view the latest releases. The development of cinema was deplored by many politicians and religious leaders. In the United

States in 1907, twenty-six million Americans went to the movies every week. By the time America entered the Second World War in 1941, weekly admissions had risen to eighty million. Movies were believed to have a damaging effect on the young. And the cinema's potential to bring about social change was of great interest and concern to the Establishment.

During the early years of the twentieth century the prudish attitudes of the nineteenth century still prevailed, and religious and political censorship were practised all over the globe. But gradually the limits on what was acceptable in the arts would alter as sexual morals changed; religion would cease to be the cornerstone of many societies; and the experiences of two world wars would radically challenge many of the old convictions.

Crowds queue outside a London cinema during the Second World War. While many people believed that cinema had a bad effect on the young, films made in wartime were often propaganda tools, used by governments to keep spirits up.

THE ROLE OF THE MEDIA

In some countries, all forms of media are controlled by the government. In other democratically-run countries, there is a free press. However, this so-called free press has many, often subtle restrictions imposed on it. Throughout the twentieth century, censorship has been applied to the media in democratically-run countries in many ways. It is not just governments that stop stories: newspaper proprietors and journalists act as censors too.

For the first two decades of the century, British and American newspapers were in good shape, reflecting a wide range of viewpoints. Although politicians and the middle classes were appalled at the popular papers aimed at the working class, more people were reading papers than ever before. Journalists exposed the ills of society and the publishers provided a vehicle for their views. The invention of the telephone and radio brought people in touch with world affairs, and there was discussion and debate about matters of state throughout Europe and North America.

Despite this liberal atmosphere some views were thought to be a step too far. In 1914 Margaret Sanger started *The Woman Rebel* – a feminist newspaper advocating the use of birth control. After five issues it was stopped by the United States Post Office, which had the authority to censor the press at the time.

Reading a state-controlled newspaper in China. In most undemocratic countries, newspapers are produced by the government, which controls what is written.

OPINION

'Freedom of the press is guaranteed only to those who own one.' Joseph Liebling, US commentator, in the *New Yorker* magazine, 1960.

When East and West Berlin were separated by the Berlin Wall during the Cold War, people who lived in East Berlin looked to Western papers for uncensored news.

GOVERNMENT AND THE MEDIA

The sign of a thriving democracy is a free press reflecting many opinions, some of which may be critical of the government. Democratic governments prefer to persuade the press rather than censor it. This uneasy alliance between the media and government has existed throughout the century, with the press often policing its own ranks.

In Britain, the British Broadcasting Corporation is financed by a licence fee paid by every television owner (formerly it was paid by everyone who owned a radio). The licence fee is set by the government; it has therefore over the years been used as a lever of government influence. In 1935 the BBC wanted to broadcast a series of talks about the British constitution. They proposed to include reference to the fascist leader Oswald Mosley and the Communist leader Harry Pollitt. The Foreign Office objected to the inclusion of Pollitt. The BBC was advised to heed this objection because negotiations over setting the next year's licence fee were just beginning. They asked the government to go public over the Pollitt ban, but it refused. Eventually, the entire series was dropped without the public ever knowing about the row.

KEY MOMENT

D Notices
In Britain in 1911, the system of D Notices was introduced. Any information covered by a D Notice was not to be published. It was argued that non-publication of such information was 'in the national interest'. The D Notices system was never ratified by parliament; it was an unofficial agreement between the media and the government. Such was the secrecy with which D Notices were surrounded that the British public did not know the system existed until 1962.

KEY MOMENT

The abdication of Edward VIII

In 1936 the British King Edward VIII was in love with an American woman, Wallis Simpson. At the time, Mrs Simpson was married to her second husband. The British government and the newspaper owners prevented anything on this matter from appearing in the press. When Wallis Simpson divorced her husband, again the British press were silent on the matter, and foreign newspapers imported into Britain were censored. But parliament decided that the British people would not accept a twice-divorced woman as their queen, and Edward, who refused to give her up, was forced to abdicate.

Edward VIII and Wallis Simpson, who became the Duke and Duchess of Windsor after Edward's abdication. News of their affair was censored by the British government.

In Japan the press was relatively free until 1931, when Japan annexed the Chinese province of Manchuria. After this the government began to 'bend' the editorials in Japanese newspapers. In 1939 the government set up its own information committee and, together with the state news agency, Domes, manipulated the press until the end of the Second World War. A large number of newspapers were suppressed altogether: in 1937 there were 1,200, but by 1945 only forty-seven remained. After the war, the occupation administration tried to remove from the press all those suspected of responsibility for the conflict. Hundreds of 'war criminals' were sacked. But in 1950, after a reversal of occupation policies, these people were given back their jobs in an effort to reduce Communist influence in the press. Some 700 Communist sympathisers were fired.

In 1960 the editors of the US newspaper the *Nation* tried to interest the major news media in articles about American preparations to invade Cuba. The *New York Times* dismissed their claims as 'shrill... anti-American propaganda'. President John Kennedy had persuaded the *Times* to withhold the story. The resulting US invasion of Cuba – known as the Bay of Pigs – was a national disaster. Afterwards, Kennedy told journalists: 'If you had printed more about the operation, you would have saved us from a colossal mistake.'

Possibly the oddest example of media censorship by government took place in Britain during the late 1980s. Under a government ban, the voices of members of Sinn Fein, a legal party linked to the banned Irish Republican Army, were not allowed to be broadcast on radio or television. Sinn Fein representatives were permitted to be seen on television and quoted in newspapers, but their words on

television and radio had to be spoken by actors. While the National Union of Journalists fought the ban as far as the European Court of Human Rights, most of the British press supported the ban as part of the fight against terrorism.

There is always tension between what governments would like to see reported and what reporters write and take pictures of. Here a photographer is stopped by police in Berlin.

However, the argument for a completely free press can be problematic. A desire to reflect the diverse nature of society has resulted in papers being started up by people with extreme views, often inciting racial or religious hatred. In the United States, the rights of such people have been upheld, often by those who strongly disagree with their views. In the US the principle of free speech is paramount. In Britain the fight for press freedom has never been as strong as in the United States. British journalists tend to support the status quo and believe that extreme ideas are unacceptable. Also the 1976 Race Relations Act made it an offence to incite hatred against people because of their ethnic origin.

OPINION

'A free press is not a privilege, but an organic necessity in a free society.' Walter Lippman, US journalist, 1965.

THE POWER OF THE OWNERS

Throughout the century, newspaper owners have wielded tremendous influence. These proprietors have determined the political stance taken by their papers. And, by choosing what to print and what not to print, they have controlled the flow of information to their readers. In 1947, the United States Commission on Freedom of the Press reported that free speech was not in danger from the government but from those who controlled access to the media.

In the USA the press has generally tried to appear impartial because its owners have been afraid of narrowing the readership by clinging to one political party. Many European newspapers, however, have made no attempts to disguise their political leanings. In Britain in 1914, Conservative Central Office provided nearly half the money to buy the *Observer*. In the 1930s, Lord Rothermere used the fourteen newspapers he owned, which included the *Daily Mail*, as outlets for his support for European fascism.

After its defeat in the Second World War, Germany was divided into zones controlled by different allied powers. The differences between US and British journalism became clear from the different press structures that were set up. In the British zone, newspapers were licensed to groups supporting one of the new legal political parties. In the US zone, each paper had to have an editorial committee of all available parties – including, sometimes, Communists.

Traditionally most of the popular British papers, such as the *Daily Express* and *Daily Mail*, have supported the Conservative Party; a

---

KEY MOMENT

Censorship for business interests

In 1997, the publishers HarperCollins commissioned Chris Patten, the last British Governor of Hong Kong, to write his autobiography. At the time HarperCollins' owner, Rupert Murdoch, was trying to buy into the Chinese media market. When he realized that Patten's book was likely to be critical of the Chinese, Murdoch 'outlined the negative aspects of publication' to the British boss of HarperCollins, and the contract was terminated.

Rupert Murdoch, owner of News Corporation, one of the five biggest media organizations in the world.

few, like the *Daily Mirror,* have supported the Labour Party. The *Sun* newspaper supported the Labour Party until it was bought by media magnate Rupert Murdoch in the 1970s. It then became a rabble-rousing right-wing paper, strongly supporting the Conservatives. When Tony Blair became leader of the Labour Party in 1994 he decided that he needed the support of the *Sun* to oust the Conservatives from power. He succeeded in wooing Rupert Murdoch to the Labour cause and went on to win the 1997 general election.

A news-stand in Italy, where the bulk of magazines and newspapers are owned by a few powerful individuals.

At the beginning of the century, most newspapers were family businesses. Now they are often part of national, or even multinational media empires. Enormous influence rests in the hands of a few people. In Germany in 1978, the Springer organization had a huge influence on the press. In some areas of Germany it controlled sixty per cent of the circulation, and on Sundays it had a complete monopoly. It owned both the powerful *Die Welt* and the largest circulation tabloid *Bild-Zeitung.* In the United States, at the end of the century, fewer than twenty corporations controlled most of the nation's mass media. Five organizations dominated the world media, with Time Warner Inc battling Rupert Murdoch's News Corporation for the top slot.

Coverage of the Ethiopian famine

By the 1980s, the western media was 'bored' with hunger in African countries. Famine was considered a non-story because it happened all the time. In 1984, the ABC TV News correspondent in Rome was told that millions of lives were threatened by drought and famine in Africa. ABC headquarters in New York decided not to cover the story because it was too expensive. Michael Buerk of the BBC went to Ethiopia and captured on film the stark reality of children starving to death. People throughout the world saw the coverage and responded, including Bob Geldof who organized a series of Live Aid fund-raising concerts. Apparently the worldwide response saved some seven million Ethiopian lives. But millions of people died before the television cameras arrived.

NEWS VALUES

To an extent, journalists control what is and what is not printed in the papers. Journalists choose which stories to include by deciding what is 'news'. In the early part of the twentieth century, the appalling living and working conditions of the poor were often covered in the American newspapers. But as competition for readers became intense in many North American cities, there was a rush for 'hot' news. The stunt and the crusade replaced liberal causes. An example of this is the *Kansas City Star*, whose editor increased the circulation by exposing the misdeeds of city officials.

The press has always been interested in the private lives of celebrities. The Hollywood studios usually tried to keep the excesses of their stars under wraps. Homosexual actors often made heterosexual marriages to keep their sexual orientation secret. Publicists fed the journalists positive news stories to keep them at bay.

An Ethiopian mother and baby, who were among the millions affected by the 1984 famine. News coverage alerted people to the disaster, and led to enormous amounts of money being raised for food.

In France a privacy law was introduced so that the private lives of well known people remained secret. President Francois Mitterand, for example, had a child by his long-time mistress, but no French newspaper could allude to the existence of her or the child.

However, in Britain and the United States the press became ever more interested in people's private lives. The fairy-tale wedding of Prince Charles to Lady Diana Spencer gave the British royal family world-class celebrity status. When the details of the breakdown of the marriage became known, stories were aired daily. There was intense media scrutiny of Prince Charles' mistress, Camilla Parker Bowles, and Princess Diana's lovers. Gone was the press restraint shown during the events leading up to the abdication of Edward VIII. The twentieth century had witnessed a dramatic shift in journalists' attitudes towards celebrity.

KEY MOMENT

Princess Diana and press intrusion

In 1997, Princess Diana was killed in a car crash in Paris when her driver lost control of the car while attempting to shake off paparazzi (photographers) on motorbikes. Diana Spencer had been pursued by the paparazzi since the end of her marriage to the Prince of Wales, when she was divested of Royal protection. In the immediate aftermath of the crash, there were calls for a privacy law to protect individuals from press harassment. But the British government was concerned that the law could be used to protect powerful people from being investigated for corruption. Plans for a privacy law were dropped.

OPINION

'There must be a privacy law. Clearly it's a form of censorship, but a form of censorship which is a human right.'
Mark Stephens, British lawyer, reacting to Princess Diana's death in 1997.

In Greece in 1996, a policeman tries to prevent Princess Diana from being mobbed by photographers.

CENSORSHIP IN WARTIME

Governments justify censorship in wartime on the grounds that the enemy may make use of information. But governments know that wars are not only won on the battlefield: they also need the full support of the people back home. For most of the twentieth century it was assumed that journalists covering a war would be part of the propaganda machine, rather than just independent witnesses. This was as true of the Gulf War (1990-91) as it was of the First World War (1914-18).

The British invented military censorship in 1856, after critical despatches appeared in *The Times* about the war against Russia in the Crimea. This negative publicity helped to bring down the government of the day. At the beginning of the First World War, Britain, France and Russia were pitted against Germany and Austria-Hungary. The British government decided to control the news coverage by allowing only six correspondents to report from the Front.

Soldiers' letters home were censored during the First World War.

NOTHING is to be written on this side except the date and signature of the sender. Sentences not required may be erased. If anything else is added the post card will be destroyed.

I have been admitted into hospital.

and am going on well.

wounded

Telegram „

parcel „

Letters follows at first opportunity.

Signature Only.

Date 22/7/15

(Postage must be prepaid on any letter or post card addressed to the sender of this card.)

The journalists wore officers' uniforms and were treated as members of the army. They had to sign the Official Secrets Act (see page 29), but there was little reason to doubt their loyalty; they felt part of the war effort and were there to provide the public with colourful stories of heroism. In order to safeguard the reputations of the generals and ensure that there was no criticism of the conduct of the campaign, the journalists happily censored their own writings. As the soldiers' letters were heavily censored too, at first all the news from the Front was good. But this began to change when the soldiers returned home on leave. As the soldiers began to check what they knew against what they read in the papers, the propaganda was exposed. The public lost confidence in the reliability of the press.

In 1917 the United States joined the war. The US government passed the Espionage Act in 1917 and the Sedition Act in 1918. These made it a crime to cause insubordination in the military or say anything disloyal about the government. US President Woodrow Wilson authorized the formation of the Committee on Public Information (CPI). This was basically a propaganda machine. Most newspapers published all 6,000 of the press releases sent out by the CPI news division during the two years that the United States was in the war.

The allied war correspondents remained loyal throughout the war. However, on 11 November 1918, the day peace was declared, journalist George Seldes broke regulations, drove into Germany and interviewed Field Marshall Hindenburg. He reported that the United States infantry attack in the Argonne had won the war, otherwise Germany would have held out longer. This story was stopped by military censors – with the support of other journalists, who were angry that they had been scooped – merely because Seldes had broken the rules.

KEY MOMENT

The imprisonment of Eugene Debs

In 1918 Eugene V Debs, who was standing for US president as Socialist Party candidate, visited three prisoners serving time for helping draft dodgers. In a subsequent speech Debs said: 'They were paying the penalty for seeking to pave the way for better conditions for all mankind.' He was found guilty of trying to obstruct the enlistment of servicemen and sentenced to ten years in prison. Debs argued that his right to free speech was being violated, but the US Supreme Court ruled against him.

During the First World War, news was censored. The terrible conditions at the Front only became known when soldiers returned home on leave.

In 1939 Britain and France declared war on Germany when Nazi forces invaded Poland. The British government recreated the successful censorship strategy of the previous war. Again allied journalists believed this to be a just war, and willingly complied with the censors. A committee met every Friday night to make up about forty propaganda lies which were repeated in the newspapers. The British government described the war correspondent as 'an integral and essential part of our fighting activities on land, on the sea and in the air.'

When the USA entered the war in 1941, President Franklin D Roosevelt created the United States Office of Censorship. This had the authority to censor all international communications, including mail, cable and radio. At its peak, the postal section of the office had more than 10,000 employees. In general the public did not object to the pressure exerted on editors and publishers to practise voluntary co-operation with the censorship program.

THE LESSON OF VIETNAM

Censorship had been successful during the two world wars because journalists were happy for the truth to be sacrificed for a greater good: the defeat of Germany and Japan. However, the Vietnam War (1964-1975) demonstrated what could happen when journalists were not on the government's side.

After gaining independence from the French in 1954, North Vietnam became a Communist state. The USA sent troops into South Vietnam to prevent it from falling under Communist control. The First Amendment of the American constitution affirms freedom of speech for all citizens except in a national emergency. As a state of national emergency – or war, in other words – was never declared in Vietnam, there could be no censorship. Correspondents were free to travel wherever they wished and write what they liked. The military tried to persuade them to support the war and used its political clout in Washington to try and influence editors at home.

At first US journalists supported the war, but when they decided that government policy was wrong, they said so. The Vietnam War was the first television war. Graphic pictures were beamed into homes around the world every night, showing the bloody brutality of war and the suffering of the Vietnamese. These, combined with news coverage of young soldiers being brought home in body bags, sapped the American public's support for the war and the United States pulled out. The American people had decided that they did not agree with their government's actions, largely as a result of its inability to control the media.

OPINION

'Maybe the historians will agree that the reporters and the cameras were decisive in the end. They brought the issue of the war to the people, before the Congress or the courts, and forced the withdrawal of US power from Vietnam.'
James Reston in the *New York Times*, 30 April 1975.

During the Vietnam War, journalists were able to travel unhindered. This CBS camera crew is interviewing American soldiers in 1967.

KEY MOMENT

The sinking of the Belgrano

When the Argentine warship, the *General Belgrano*, was sunk by the British navy off the coast of Argentina in 1982, the British government refused to release much information. The Argentines argued that the vessel had not been heading towards the war zone as the government suggested, but retreating from it. The log book from the British vessel which sunk the *Belgrano* was conveniently 'lost'.

NEWS MANAGEMENT

In 1982, Argentina invaded the British-governed Falkland Islands (or Malvinas, as Argentines call them). Britain sent a task force of warships to win the islands back. By the time war had been declared on Argentina, the Ministry of Defence (MoD) had honed its plan to manage the news. The lesson of Vietnam was heeded: all journalists were kept under control. As every journalist had to travel with the task force, the MoD controlled access to the battlefield.

All correspondents had to agree to censorship at source before they were allowed to travel, and all telecommunications from the task force and the islands were controlled by the military. While live coverage of many world events was by this time commonplace, most of the war journalists' reports were held for at least twenty-four hours, and sometimes for three or four days, before being released.

The censors suppressed bad news, or released it in dribs and drabs to nullify its impact. At its daily briefings, the MoD successfully projected itself as the only source of accurate information about events. Many journalists did not feel part of the war effort, but they were only able to express their views when they returned home after the war was over. By this time Britain had defeated Argentina.

During the Gulf War, news of casualties was carefully managed.

In 1990, Iraqi forces invaded Kuwait, an action which prompted the USA and Britain to declare war on Iraq. During the Gulf War the censors sought to convince the public that new technology had removed the horrors of battle. Reports of 'surgical' air strikes, bombs dropped with 'pin-point accuracy' and the 'taking out' of military targets involved little or no 'collateral damage' (dead civilians). The censors painted a picture of war without death. Human casualties were not seen on television until weeks after the start of the war.

These Bosnian children and their grandfather are in a refugee camp after fleeing from Serbian troops. Despite the propaganda to the contrary, in war women, children and older people are often those who suffer most.

Most of the journalists were loyal to the military who, in turn, allowed correspondents the live broadcasting they demanded. America's twenty-four hour news service, CNN, had a correspondent based in Iraq. Many commentators in Britain and the United States believed that he should not have been allowed to broadcast from Baghdad for fear that he was disseminating enemy propaganda. Even as an independent witness he was suspect.

Throughout the century, governments in war have learned how important it is to control the information available and to have support from journalists, or at least from their editors. Also, as communications technology has become increasingly sophisticated, the censors have adapted it for propaganda use. The winning of hearts and minds at home is paramount in the wartime propaganda battle.

KEY MOMENT

Attack on British soldiers

During the Gulf War, British soldiers were fired on and killed by American aircraft. Correspondents and the soldiers' families were told that the attack was at night and in bad weather conditions. After the end of the war, investigations showed that the attack had taken place during the day in cloudless skies.

CENSORSHIP AND NATIONAL SECURITY

OPINION

'Congress shall make no law abridging the freedom of speech, or of the press.'
First Amendment to the US constitution, 1792.

Throughout the twentieth century, Britain and the United States have prided themselves on the freedom of their citizens, a freedom limited only in times of crisis when political censorship is necessary to protect the people. The First Amendment to the American constitution guarantees each citizen freedom of speech. It has been used time and again in court cases, giving liberty to cause offence as well as to dissent. However, during the century people in Britain and the USA have had to fight for freedom against their governments. These battles have not always resulted in a successful outcome for the citizens, or for freedom of speech.

The American judge, Oliver Wendell Holmes, who first ruled that free speech is not an absolute right.

OPINION

'In the UK, government information is generally kept secret unless there is a good reason why it should be available, while in the USA information is generally available unless there is a good reason why it should be kept secret.'
Christian Wolmar,
Censorship, 1990.

In 1919 the American judge Oliver Wendell Holmes ruled that the First Amendment does not protect all speech. Famously, he argued: 'The most stringent protection of free speech would not protect a man in falsely shouting "fire" in a theatre and causing a panic.... The question in every case is whether the words used are used in such circumstances and are of such a nature as to create a clear and present danger that they will bring about the substantive evils that Congress has a right to prevent.' This means that the right to freedom of speech in the United States must be weighed against other rights. The history of censorship in the USA in the twentieth century is the battle between free speech and restrictions, such as threats to national security.

There has been greater importance attached to keeping government information secret in Britain than most other western democracies. In 1938, the auction house Sotheby's was prevented from selling the original letters of Lord Nelson, the heroic admiral at the Battle of Trafalgar in 1805, to the Duke of Wellington. The government ruled them official secrets. And in 1958, two Oxford graduates were sent to prison for detailing their experiences of national service (one year's military service which was compulsory at the time).

KEY MOMENT

The Official Secrets Act
In 1911, the British government passed the Official Secrets Act. This made the unauthorized disclosure of any official information a crime punishable by a jail sentence. It meant that all information a person working for the government came across, whether the menu for the canteen or a politically sensitive document, was deemed to be 'official', whatever its real importance.

Postal censors at work in Britain at the start of the Second World War. It was generally accepted that the rigorous censorship applied during the war would be lifted in peacetime.

OPINION

'In the future days, which we seek to make secure, we look forward to a world founded on four essential human freedoms. The first is freedom of speech and expression – everywhere in the world.'
US President Franklin D Roosevelt, 1941.

Jack Warner, Vice-President of Warner Brothers, gives evidence to the HUAC in Washington.

In the United States, the House Un-American Activities Committee (HUAC) was created in 1938 to 'expose Communist infiltration' in the Congress of Industrial Organizations (the body to which all the trade unions belonged) and in the government itself. After the Second World War, as Communist governments took control of many eastern European countries, and Communism was perceived to be a potent force in Asia and Latin America, the USA became even more worried about its influence. In 1945, Senator Joseph McCarthy began an anti-Communist crusade. He accused the State Department of harbouring 205 prominent Communists, a charge he was unable to substantiate. He also said that the State Department had Communist books in libraries in Washington and all over the world. Some forty

titles were removed, including *The Selected Works of Thomas Jefferson* (a former American president) and *The Children's Hour* by Lillian Hellman.

McCarthy took over the House Un-American Activities Committee and used it to try and hunt down Communists and sympathisers in all walks of life. One of the areas it concentrated on was the arts, in particular the Hollywood film industry. Many prominent actors, writers and directors were brought before the committee to inform on their friends, or 'name names'. At no stage was membership of the Communist Party illegal; nevertheless some people were jailed and others were blacklisted so that they could not work. Dozens of people who were blacklisted found their contracts terminated and their careers broken. Some could only find work under assumed names, or abroad.

COURT INJUNCTIONS AND RESTRAINING ORDERS

Sometimes government efforts to keep certain information secret are thwarted by journalists. In this event another tool of censorship is used – a court injunction or restraining order against the press publishing the material. The First Amendment was most severely tested politically in the case of the Pentagon Papers in 1971. The US government tried to prevent the *New York Times* and *Washington Post* from publishing classified documents about the Vietnam War. The court ruled that under certain circumstances where publication might seriously interfere with foreign policy or affect the ability of the US government to conduct a war, publication might be prevented. However, in this case the Supreme Court ruled that the government had to prove that the release of secret documents would lead to 'direct, immediate and irreparable harm' to the running of the country before a newspaper could be prevented from printing them.

OPINION

'The Un-American Activities Committee had provided me with the desire to make its like impossible here any more, and maybe on some far off day, everywhere else in the world.'
Arthur Miller, playwright, explaining why he accepted the international presidency of PEN – an association of writers against censorship.

KEY MOMENT

US Freedom of Information Act
In 1966 the US Freedom of Information Act was passed (it was strengthened in 1974). With it, Congress established the American people's right to know. The Act gathered a growing list of exemptions which made it possible for the government to retain secrets. Under presidents Ronald Reagan and George Bush, officials were encouraged to find ways to get round the Act. Today it can be extremely time-consuming for the public and press to use it. However it makes a difference: European journalists often use the Act to find out information that is blocked by their own governments, but published in the United States.

THE SPYCATCHER AFFAIR

In the 1980s Peter Wright, a former member of the British secret service, published a book of his memoirs, *Spycatcher*, which was immediately banned in the UK. *Spycatcher* outlined a series of incredible actions carried out by spies working for the government, including phone-tapping, bugging and propaganda wars against the USSR and even allies such as France. It even detailed secret service preparations for a *coup* attempt against the Labour government in the mid-1970s.

The British government opposed the publication of *Spycatcher* because Peter Wright had broken his oath of secrecy and they were worried that other retired spies would do likewise. It also maintained that the secret service could not function if details of its operations were to be made public a decade later. In a court case in Australia, where the British government was also trying to prevent publication, Sir Robert Armstrong, the most senior civil servant in Britain, was forced to admit that he had been 'economical with the truth'. The government tried to prevent Peter Wright's allegations from being reported in the British press. The newspapers only won their case after taking it to the European Court of Human Rights.

The memoirs of former British secret service agent, Peter Wright, on sale in New York. In 1998 another agent, David Shayler, also went public about the secret service. He subsequently went into hiding in Paris. The French refused to extradite him to Britain to stand trial for breaking the Official Secrets Act.

People who disclose government secrets can suffer terribly for their actions. While working for the Israeli nuclear research facility, Mordechai Vanunu discovered that Israel was secretly making nuclear weapons. In 1986 he took his story to a British newspaper, *The Sunday Times*. When the article was published, Vanunu was kidnapped by the Israeli secret service and sentenced to eighteen years' solitary confinement. For almost twelve years he was imprisoned alone in a tiny, concrete cell.

THE SKOKIE CASE

Liberals in the United States had always believed that the First Amendment would enable them to criticize and question the government. However, towards the end of the twentieth century the First Amendment was increasingly used to protect racists and others intent on spreading hate. The Skokie case was one such example. The Supreme Court ruled that the First Amendment protected neo-Nazis who wanted to march with swastikas through a town of Holocaust survivors in Illinois. To prevent them from doing so was seen as censoring their right to free expression.

The white supremacist organization, the Ku Klux Klan also won the right to run its own radio station. This provoked debate among opponents of censorship. Does the freedom to publish and say what you want include the right to abuse other racial and ethnic groups? In the United States, supporters of the First Amendment say that there can be no limits, for as soon as a boundary is set limiting the activities of one group then other boundaries will follow. Balancing the rights of one side against the rights of another has always been an issue in the debate about political censorship.

KEY MOMENT

Burning the US flag
In 1989, 'Texas v Johnson' was the first of the famous 'flag burning' cases. Some Americans had burned the US flag in protest against the government. This was considered a crime against the state, because the US flag is held in such regard that every morning children in many schools pledge allegiance to the flag hung in their classroom. However, the judge of the Supreme Court ruled that no matter how offensive a speech is, it is protected by the First Amendment. He ruled that burning the American flag was like making a speech, and therefore protected.

The Ku Klux Klan demonstrate in the USA in 1987. Their right to march is protected by the First Amendment.

REPRESSIVE REGIMES

One lesson to be learned from history is this: the greater the repression, the greater the censorship. Over the past hundred years, many countries have been governed by dictators or totalitarian regimes. In Europe there have been dictatorships in Germany, Italy, Spain, Portugal, Greece and elsewhere. In 1917, the repressive ruler of Russia, the Tsar, was ousted in favour of a Communist dictatorship; and eastern Europe was dominated by Russia from the end of the Second World War until the collapse of Communism in 1989.

About 400,000 protestors march against the government of Augusto Pinochet in Chile in 1983. Pinochet seized power in 1973. His troops killed and tortured thousands of people who opposed his regime.

For much of the twentieth century many Latin American countries have been run by dictators. Under the old regime of apartheid in South Africa, the white minority ruled the black majority through fear and oppression. Most African countries were

colonies – governed by a European power – at the turn of the century. When the colonies gained their freedom, the new rulers often continued to use the repressive laws of their former masters. Israel has been the only democratically governed country in the Middle East this century; but the Israeli state does not allow the Arabs who live in Israel to be citizens, and they have few rights. In South-East Asia few political dissidents have been allowed to express themselves openly, and dictatorships have flourished.

SPREADING DISSENT

In all these countries, the fight against censorship, whether literary or more overtly political, has been a fight against repression. There is enormous fear of the written word because it is the most powerful way to spread criticism and ideas. The typewriter and the duplicating machine have been used all over the world to spread dissent. Under Communism, eastern European dissidents would type out their stories and articles, make carbon copies and pass them round by hand. In Czechoslovakia in 1972, any person buying a typewriter had to have their name and address and a sample of type registered with the secret police. In Saddam Hussein's Iraq, a licence is needed to buy a typewriter.

The leaders of authoritarian regimes are always determined to stamp out dissent. Although they use censorship to maintain the system, they argue that it exists to protect the people. Dissent is always portrayed as an attempt (often under the influence of a foreign power) to destabilize the state. For example, in Argentina, under the dictator Juan Perón, publications were banned because they were considered immoral or pro-Communist. In 1949 the leading daily newspaper *La Prensa* was seized by Perón's officials. It was not returned to its owners until 1955. In 1976 a period of book censorship began, and scholars were persecuted for their ideas.

KEY MOMENT

Press censorship under Communism

In 1917, Bolshevik leader Vladimir Ilyich Lenin ordered the closure of newspapers which advocated resistance to the new authorities or attempted to 'sow disorder by the publication of clearly slanderous mis-statements of facts'. There was a civil war between the 'reds' (Communists) and the 'whites' (Russians who wanted a return to Tsarist rule). Lenin said that the closure was temporary and promised that, on the return to normal order, complete freedom of the press would be restored. But press censorship was never lifted under Communism.

REVOLUTION IN RUSSIA

At the beginning of the century, Russia was ruled by Tsar Nicholas II who employed a vast network of secret police to ensure that there was no dissent among his people. In 1907, 175 journalists were jailed and 413 periodicals banned for breaking Russia's strict censorship rules. In 1917, revolutionaries – some Communist, some socialist and some just anti-Tsar – ousted Nicholas. For a short time there was freedom from censorship, but it was not long before the ruling Bolsheviks realized that this meant their enemies could say and print what they wanted.

Molotov, Stalin and Lenin in the editorial offices of the revolutionary newspaper, Pravda.

In 1922, the Chief Administration for Literary Affairs and Publishing, known as GLAVIT, was set up. GLAVIT employed 70,000 people and oversaw a program of censorship throughout the country. All publications were read by the censor and there was a 300-page index of banned subjects. One of the first writers to be banned was Yergeny Zamyatin who wrote *W*, a forerunner to George Orwell's *Animal Farm*.

As the Bolsheviks consolidated power in the new Soviet Union, they used institutions such as the press, radio, cinema, theatre, libraries, museums, schools and other seats of learning to spread their ideological message. On Lenin's death in 1924, Josef Stalin came to power. He saw Russia as a beleaguered nation fighting capitalism on all sides. During the early 1930s, he ensured state control of every aspect of the communications and publishing media. Under Stalin a number of writers who would not conform took their own lives, many others died in prison camps.

In 1932 the Communist Party founded the Writers' Union. This was the only professional organization of writers permitted by the state, and it ensured that all its members conformed to the wishes of the party. Any writer expelled from the union could not be published. A writer, Stalin said, was: 'the engineer of men's souls'. Writers were instructed to pen stories about the new Soviet men, to give readers a guide to exemplary behaviour. Stalin ruled that writers must show unfailing optimism and promote the victorious onward march of Soviet industrial and agricultural policies.

OPINION

'Freedom is a class concept. We Bolsheviks are not going to grant unrestricted freedom to monarchists and anarchists.'
Vladimir Ilych Lenin, 1920.

KEY MOMENT

Information ban in Russia
In 1922, Stalin ruled that journalists could not publish information on the following events without special government permission: natural disasters in the Soviet Union; fires, explosions and other disasters; price increases; and improved standards of living outside the Soviet Union.

Cheering Communist youths carry a portrait of Stalin.

DICTATORSHIPS IN EUROPE

In Portugal, the dictator Dr Antonio de Oliveira Salazar ruled from 1932 to 1968. He used censorship to try and isolate Portugal from the rest of the world. In the 1940s all photographs of barefoot children were banned, so that Portugal could not be perceived as poor or backward.

There was rigorous censorship of the press, theatre and advertising. Nothing was published or broadcast without careful and costly scrutiny. Any news stories that might alarm the public or disparage the dignity of the nation were cut and replaced with approved material. Government stories were printed as though they were editorial copy, and even the sporting press was scrutinized to ensure the correct level of patriotic fervour. Censors revised the school curriculum and teachers were carefully selected. Disloyalty or any questioning of the social order was repressed as subversion or Communism.

Spain's General Franco bids a fond farewell to Adolf Hitler in 1940. Both leaders kept a very tight control on the media.

In neighbouring Spain, the dictator General Miguel Primo de Rivera governed from 1923-1930, and enforced rigid censorship of the press. General Franco came to power in 1938 and established total control over the press, the law and the government; dissenting voices, opinions or news concerning government policies were all censored. During the Second World War, Franco supported the Nazi regime in Germany, but after Hitler's defeat he passed the 'Fuero de los Espanoles', a Spanish bill of rights, to present a respectable face to the victorious allies. Article 12 of the bill of rights said: 'All Spaniards can freely express their opinions provided they do not attack the fundamental principle of the State.' However, in practice this meant that no opinion could be expressed that was not in favour of the state and all it stood for. All public meetings were closely controlled by the Ministry of the Interior and the local civil governor. Censorship remained a central feature of the regime until 1966 and, even after that date, attacks on the government entailed fines and imprisonment.

Nazi youths burn books that have been banned under the Third Reich.

THE THIRD REICH

The most notorious dictator of the twentieth century was Adolf Hitler, leader of the National Socialist (Nazi) Party, who became Chancellor of Germany in 1933. His time in office is called the Third Reich. Within a year of coming to power, he had banned all other political parties and many newspapers. The British ambassador at the time noted that the German daily press contained a list of papers suppressed or suspended.

The establishment of a Reich Chamber of Culture meant that all journalistic, theatrical, musical and radio work was brought under Goebbels' control. Anyone making even the most cautious attempt at political criticism disappeared into a concentration camp. Those found guilty of publishing news detrimental to the public interest were severely punished.

Daily bulletins from the government informed newspapers what to report, which stories to stress and which to play down or ignore. All editors, reporters and other regular contributors were required to be members of the Reich Press Chamber and approved by the regime. Authors, artists and composers were controlled in similar ways. Some 250 writers including the world famous novelist, Thomas Mann, went into exile.

FASCISM IN ITALY

In 1919 Benito Mussolini formed the Milan *fascio* (combat troop). Within a month, Italian fascists had broken up a socialist rally and wrecked the printing plant of a socialist newspaper. In 1924, Mussolini gained control of Italy. Many Italian newspapers vehemently criticized fascism and the government, but Mussolini curbed press freedom by giving local authorities the power to suppress newspapers which published objectionable material. Many writers went into exile.

An Italian propaganda poster shows Benito Mussolini embracing a child.

After the Second World War and the defeat of Nazi Germany, the Soviet Union brought Communism to the countries of eastern Europe, most of which had previously been under fascist control. Under Soviet rule there was always dissent, not just against Communist ideology but against foreign domination too. In Hungary, Poland and Czechoslovakia, in particular, writers and other intellectuals led attempts at achieving reform. In Czechoslovakia, writers who had been banned by the Nazis found themselves banned under Communism. They included the poet Herman Chromy and the writer Jiri Wolf. Most dissident writers in eastern Europe and the Soviet Union spent some time in jail or prison camps – some were killed. Soviet journalist Victor Verkhin was arrested for investigating inadequate safety measures in Ukranian mines. He subsequently died from the beatings he received in prison.

After Stalin's death in 1953, censorship was lifted in some areas, partly because his successor, Nikita Kruschev, wanted to distance himself from the previous regime. In 1962, Kruschev ordered the publication of Alexander Solzhenitsyn's book, *A Day in the Life of Ivan Denisovich*. This detailed the horror

> **OPINION**
>
> 'Czechoslovakian history since 1948 has been presented, in the main, as the history of the Communist Party and its government, its resolutions and congresses, even its show trials. Yet that is only the tip of the iceberg, with the life of the nation continuing underneath the surface. It is this hidden face of reality that our unofficial literature has aimed to portray.'
> Jan Vladislaw, Czechoslovakian writer, 1983.

> **OPINION**
>
> 'In our country the lie has become not just a moral category but a pillar of the state.'
> Alexander Solzhenitsyn, exiled Russian writer, 1974.

Alexander Solzhenitsyn speaking in Moscow in 1998. Four years earlier he had returned to Russia after twenty years in exile.

People in Prague, Czechoslovakia, celebrate the election of former banned playwright Vaclav Havel to the presidency in 1989.

of prison camps and exposed the truth about Stalin. But Solzhenitsyn did not remain in favour for long. In 1969 he was expelled from the Writer's Union and forced to publish his books abroad, and in 1974 he was banned from the Soviet Union.

A number of Soviet writers only published abroad. Boris Pasternak's *Dr Zhivago* was first published in Italy and then banned in the Soviet Union. Pasternak was forced to refuse the Nobel Prize for Literature and condemned by the Writers' Union. He had to earn his living doing translation work.

COMMUNIST CHINA

Communist China under Mao Zedong was based on a philosophy which stressed the importance of ideology and re-education. Dissent was squashed and most literature banned. Novels were considered bourgeois or anti-revolutionary.

After Mao's death in 1976, the political and cultural policy was marginally liberalized. Some local publishers, especially those in the provinces, began to publish risqué books, such as pulp romantic novels and soft porn. This low-brow, popular literature found a

Chinese students demonstrate for democracy in Tiananmen Square, Beijing, under a portrait of Chairman Mao.

substantial market. But there were soon campaigns against spiritual pollution and bourgeois liberalism. In 1987, more than 3,000 people were arrested and millions of books, videos and magazines were confiscated in a sudden crackdown. However, China's leaders found themselves in a difficult position: China needed to open up to the rest of the world for trade purposes, but western leaders demanded some evidence of a Chinese human rights policy. There was growing dissent and movement for change.

APARTHEID IN SOUTH AFRICA

At the turn of the century, South Africa was a British colony. In 1910 it was given independence but remained part of the Commonwealth, ruled by a white minority government. In 1948 the South African government introduced a series of apartheid measures.

The government was concerned that education of the black population would breed troublemakers. In 1953 the education syllabus was changed to limit the learning of black children. Rather than developing their intellects for further education, the government recommended that they be taught practical skills. In black primary schools the teaching of English ceased, instead children were taught in Afrikaans or a 'native' language.

KEY MOMENT

Massacre in Tiananmen Square

In June 1989, students and other activists occupied Tiananmen Square in Beijing, and, in front of the world's media, demanded greater democracy. The Chinese leader, Deng Xiaoping, ordered the army tanks in and 2,600 people were massacred. This marked the end of a liberal attitude towards censorship and led to a rigid control of literature and the expression of dissident ideas. After Tiananmen Square, thousands of dissidents were rounded up all over the country, charged with counter-revolutionary activity and given long prison sentences. They included writers, publishers, journalists, academics, artists, students and workers. By 1992 there were at least 976 labour reform camps, each holding about 50,000 people.

OPINION

'What is the use of teaching a black child mathematics when he cannot use it in practice? Education must train and teach people in accordance with their opportunities in life.'
South African Prime Minister Hendrick Verwoerd, 1953.

OPINION

'I have cherished the ideal of a democratic and free society in which all persons live together in harmony. It is an ideal which I hope to live for and achieve. But if needs be it is an ideal for which I am prepared to die.'
Nelson Mandela, leader of the African National Congress, at his trial in 1962.

In 1960 the African National Congress and the Pan African Congress, two black organizations opposed to apartheid, were banned. In 1962 over one hundred people were banned from attending political meetings. During the 1960s and 1970s, the security police suppressed resistance to the regime. Increasing numbers of people among them Winnie Mandela, wife of ANC leader Nelson Mandela, were placed under house arrest, which meant that they could not leave their homes. Books were banned and many South African authors only published abroad. In 1973 Steve Biko, a founder of the South African Students' Organization which encouraged black self reliance, was served with a banning order severely restricting his movements and freedom of speech. In 1977, at the age of thirty-one, he was beaten to death while in police custody.

Of all the regimes described in this chapter, only Communist China remains. And even China is changing – at the end of the twentieth century there are suggestions that a blind eye is being turned towards political dissent in metropolitan centres like Beijing. If twentieth-century history has shown us anything, it is that a system which relies on perpetual censorship cannot expect to survive.

In South Africa a camera crew is deterred from filming around Crossroads squatter camps.

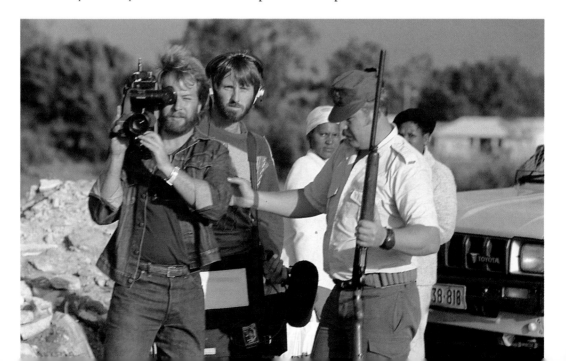

CENSORSHIP AND RELIGION

At the turn of the century, western Europe and the USA consisted of Christian countries with the majority of the population attending church. In Britain blasphemy, or the showing of contempt for God, had been a crime since 1617 when John Taylor was put in the stocks for denouncing Christ as a whoremaster and orthodox religion as a cheat. The blasphemy law – which applied only to the Christian religion – was still in existence three hundred years later. In the United States, to which many of the original settlers had escaped from religious persecution, there were no laws on religion. However, behind this supposed tolerance lurked a strain of Christian fundamentalism which sought to censor, among other things, the teaching of children in schools.

KEY MOMENT

The Scopes Monkey Trial
In 1925 John T Scopes, a young high school teacher, was arrested for violating Tennessee's law prohibiting the teaching of biological evolution (Darwinism). He was defended by the liberal attorney, Clarence Darrow, in one of the most famous courtroom confrontations in US history. Scopes was found guilty and fined $100. In an appeal to the State Supreme Court, the law forbidding lessons on evolution was upheld, but Scopes's conviction was overturned on a technicality.

Defence attorney Dudley Malone (left), John T Scopes (centre) and Clarence Darrow during the Scopes Monkey Trial in 1925.

The debate about the literal truth of the Bible and the teaching of science in schools has been going on in the southern states of the USA throughout this century. In 1924, Baptist legislators in Tennessee pushed through a bill that made it illegal for schools 'to teach any theory that denies the story of the Divine Creation of man as taught in the Bible...'. During the 1980s, fundamentalists in Tennessee claimed that the requirement that their children read certain school books violated their religious rights. In Alabama, forty-four textbooks were banned from schools for teaching 'the religion of secular humanism'.

Protestors at the opening of Martin Scorsese's film The Last Temptation of Christ. *The film was thought by some to show Jewish people in an unfair light.*

DARWINISM

Many schools in Tennessee still refuse to teach Darwinism – the view that people and apes have a common ancestor. This is because it directly contradicts the story told in the Bible, which says that on the sixth day God created man. Throughout the century, religious matters have continued to inspire firmly held views and fundamentalists have sought to silence the opposition. Fundamentalists are, by definition, intolerant of other views. Their lives are dominated by their religion. They believe that their religion is the only religion and that they are the only true followers. Fundamentalists are often extremely successful lobbyists, because they are so sure that they have moral right on their side.

In Britain successful prosecutions for blasphemy have been rare. One of the few took place in 1940 and concerned a Mr Woodhead whose passport photo showed him in swimming trunks with

his arms outstretched. He had drawn a cross on the photo, so that it bore some similarity to the Crucifixion.

However, as the twentieth century progressed, people generally felt that the blasphemy law was 'unsatisfactory and archaic' and belonged to an era in which it was felt that to reject Christianity would threaten the social order. 'The reason for this law', said Lord Denning in 1949, 'was because it was thought that a denial of Christianity was liable to shake the fabric of society, which was itself founded on Christian religion. There is no such danger to society now and the offence of blasphemy is a dead letter.'

In 1979 in Britain, the only prosecution for blasphemy since the Second World War concerned a poem in the magazine *Gay News*. The author of the poem, Professor James Kirkup, used the imagery of physical love to convey his feeling of union with God. He was given a suspended jail sentence, which was quashed on appeal.

Members of the fundamentalist Taliban militia in Afghanistan. Since the Taliban have been in power they have enforced strict religious rules. These include forbidding women to work and girls to be educated.

THE SATANIC VERSES

However, the publication in 1988 of *The Satanic Verses* caused worldwide controversy. Muslims found it deeply offensive and attacked the author, Salman Rushdie, for sacrilege and blasphemy. Copies of the book were burnt in many Islamic countries and by Muslims in Britain. On 14 February 1989, the Muslim leader of Iran, the Ayatollah Khomeini, issued a *fatwa* or death sentence on Rushdie. During the twelve months after the *fatwa* was issued, the publishers, Penguin Books, received death threats, twelve British bookshops were firebombed and many were threatened. Salman Rushdie went into hiding for his own safety. British Muslims demanded that British blasphemy law be extended to other religions.

In London, Muslims demonstrate against Salman Rushdie and his publisher, Penguin Books.

There were worldwide campaigns both in favour of and against Rushdie. Writers, academics and others opposed to censorship campaigned for an end to the *fatwa*. *The Satanic Verses* was banned in all Islamic countries and other African countries, including Kenya. However, some writers and commentators believed that Rushdie had knowingly offended Muslims and thought that he should have censored himself. In 1998 Iran lifted the *fatwa*, but some extremist Islamic groups still offered a reward for Rushdie's death.

Salman Rushdie's case was not an isolated incident. In 1998, feminist author Taslima Nasrin went into hiding in her native Bangladesh after Muslim extremists offered a $5000 reward for her death. They believed that Nasrin had called for a revision of the Q'uran, the Islamic Holy Book. However Nasrin argued that she was misquoted, and had only called for changes in the strict rules that limit Bangladeshi women to housework and childrearing.

In the 1990s in the USA, the 'Impression' reading series came under attack. While some teachers and parents considered that the books sparked students' interest in reading, others believed that they contravened their religious beliefs. A section on Hallowe'en, which included ghost and goblin stories, was attacked for teaching witchcraft.

Towards the end of the twentieth century, the numbers of both Christian and Islamic fundamentalists have increased considerably. In the next century we must decide where to draw the line between avoiding offence to people's passionately held beliefs and the principles of free speech.

OPINION

'What he [Salman Rushdie] has written is far worse to Muslims than if he'd raped one's own daughter. It's an assault on every Muslim's inner being.... It's like a knife being dug into you or being raped yourself.'
Dr Zaki Badawi, Chairman of the British Islamic Law Council.

OPINION

'The idea of extending the offence of blasphemy to cover all religions would require a tight legal definition of what is religion and could open up a nightmare of endless court cases which, if they succeeded, would silence all humanists, atheists, heretics and free-thinkers.'
Tony Benn, British member of parliament, 1989.

Taslima Nasrin in a Paris hotel in 1994 at the start of four years of self-imposed exile. Nasrin left her native Bangladesh because of a death threat by Islamic militants. She returned to Bangladesh in 1998, but lives in hiding.

CENSORSHIP AND SEX

The twentieth century has seen dramatic changes in attitudes towards sex. At the beginning of the century the sexual climate was very different. Heads of Victorian households would order piano legs to be covered up because they were thought to be lewd. And the sight of a well-turned ankle under a woman's dress was thought to be enough to make a man's head spin.

In spite of this, the definition of obscenity has remained unchanged throughout the century. Censorship of sexual matters was supposed to protect the vulnerable. Those who sought to stop obscene books and plays considered themselves morally virtuous and upstanding, while the authors and artists viewed them as straight-laced puritans.

The uncut version of Lady Chatterley's Lover *went on sale in November 1960. In this posed photo, a reader attracts interest on the London Underground.*

Although there is far more openness about sex now, the debate about what is acceptable has raged throughout the century. And in the United States in particular, the debate about pornography – obscene writing or pictures – is still extremely fierce.

The banning of Radclyffe Hall's book *The Well of Loneliness* was one of the few big test cases during the first part of the century. By and large, publishers knew what was acceptable and made sure that their authors stuck to it. However, D H Lawrence's novel *The Rainbow* was withdrawn and destroyed in 1915 for being too obscene. When his *Lady Chatterley's Lover* was published in 1928, most of the more controversial passages had been cut by the editor. It was not until 1960, when the unexpurgated version was published by Penguin, that the book was prosecuted for obscenity. The prosecution was not upheld. Occasionally literary merit could save a book from censorship. In 1934, James Joyce's *Ulysses* escaped prosecution on those grounds. But this was not the case with E M Forster's *Maurice*, written in 1915. The novel, which features a homosexual relationship, was withheld from publication until the 1960s.

> ## KEY MOMENT
> ### The Well of Loneliness
> In 1928, Radclyffe Hall's novel *The Well of Loneliness* was banned for being obscene. A story with a lesbian theme, it came to grief on one sentence: 'And that night they were not divided.' The British Attorney General Sir Thomas Inksip said: 'The book seeks to glorify a vice or to produce a plea of toleration for those who practise it.... It is propaganda.' The case was not tried in front of a jury for fear that they would be swayed by an articulate defence. The 1929 obscenity trial in the United States failed, and the British ban was eventually lifted in 1949. The papers from the trial were due to be released publicly in 1998, but the British government maintained that they still constituted a threat to national security. The trial papers will not now be released until 2007.

Egypt's President Nasser appointed five housewives to censor every film to ensure that family interests were preserved on screen. A woman cuts an offending scene in 1966.

KEY MOMENT

The Hays Code

William Harrison Hays was US Postmaster General and president of the Motion Pictures Producers and Distributors of America. In 1934 that association introduced a system of rigid self-censorship, the so-called Production Code, that came to be known as the Hays Code. Because of their powerful effect on audiences, motion pictures attracted the close attention of the censors. The Code laid down strict rules about representing sexual relationships on screen; these included separate beds for married couples. If a screen kiss lasted more than thirty seconds it was rated obscene. Film-makers used all sorts of devices to get round the Code. Director Cecil B DeMille adapted stories from the Bible to get scenes of orgy, rape, depravity and perversion past the censors. The Hays Code ran until 1968, when film classification was introduced.

In the United States, groups opposing the censorship of sexually explicit material tried to use the First Amendment – which guaranteed freedom of speech – to stop prosecutions. But it was not until after the Second World War that US courts began seriously to consider whether sexual expression should be treated in the same way as religious or political expression, and therefore be protected by the constitution.

In the mid-1960s the so-called sexual revolution took place. Sexually explicit material became more acceptable in western society and found a wider market. The musical *Hair* included reference to sex, drugs and the Vietnam War, and involved the whole cast taking off their clothes. It played in New York before transferring to London. Until 1967 in England, all plays had to be licensed before being put on. This meant that the script had to be approved. Sex was a sensitive subject and playwrights, knowing that they had to tread carefully, mostly censored themselves.

Will Hays greets news photographers in 1922. As president of the Motion Picture Producers and Distributors of America, he introduced the system of self-censorship known as the Hays Code in 1934.

The three Oz editors (Richard Neville is in the centre) on their release from prison in 1971.

After 1967, when the requirement was finally dropped, there was an abundance of nudity on stage. Plays like *O Calcutta!* were a reaction to what had gone before. By the end of the 1990s, nudity on stage was so normal that it rarely raised comment.

UNDERGROUND MAGAZINES

The 1960s also saw the publication of a number of 'underground' magazines, such as *Ink*, *Black Dwarf* and *Oz*. These were published by young people and carried many articles about sex. They reflected changing attitudes, covering topics like contraception, abortion and sex before marriage. While they concerned issues that were being talked about by young people, they were also intended to shock the older generation.

Sexually explicit films began to be shown more widely from the late-1960s. In many countries there was an inevitable backlash against this increased frankness. In the USA action was taken under the obscenity laws, with Boston the most active locality in attempting to suppress objectionable matter. Other countries took a more liberal approach: in Belgium, Denmark and Uruguay there was no pre-censorship of films for adults.

KEY MOMENT

The *Oz* trial

In Britain in 1970, Richard Neville the editor of the underground magazine, *Oz*, was found guilty of intent 'to debauch and corrupt the morals of children and young persons within the realm and implant in their minds lustful and perverted desires.' Neville had brought out a special 'School Kids' issue, 'put together with the help and inspiration of about twenty young people, all 18 or under.' The *Oz* prosecution was important because underground magazines deliberately set out to shock the Establishment and appeal to rebellious young people. For the Establishment and many members of the older generation, it was a chance to strike back.

PORNOGRAPHY

In 1968, US President Lyndon Johnson appointed an obscenity commission to look at the seriousness of the traffic in pornography and its effects on society. The commission found no cause for alarm, but when, in the same year, Richard Nixon became president the US Senate repudiated these findings.

By 1985, when the US Attorney General's Commission on Pornography, known as the Meese Commission, was set up, the battle lines had been drawn. Booksellers, libertarians and pornographers stood on one side; Evangelical Christians, right-wingers and certain feminists on the other. The Meese Commission listened to testimony by 'victims' of pornography and police from vice and morals squads who were testifying as experts on child molestation and the harmful effects of pornography.

Before the findings were published, the Executive Director of the Commission wrote to businesses, such as K Mart and the Southland Corporation. He accused them of being the nation's largest purveyors of pornography because they distributed *Playboy* and *Penthouse* magazines. Many stores succumbed and withdrew the magazines from sale. *Playboy* and the American Booksellers' Association subsequently sued the Meese Commission, and won.

In the West, certain feminists have fought to outlaw pornography because they believe it demeans women. In Britain, the MP Clare Short tried to ban tabloid newspaper pictures of bare-breasted women. In the United States there was an attempt to make publishers liable for criminal damages if a rapist or other criminal convinces a jury that pornography contributed to his actions. The anti-pornography feminists maintain that pornography contributes to the general cultural environment in which women are treated as sex objects. In the 1980s, Andrea Dworkin

Protestors against pornography in Times Square, New York City.

and Catherine McKinnon, two American feminist anti-pornography campaigners argued that pornography causes violence against women. They said that the victims of such violence should sue the publishers of the magazines, the bookshops which stock the magazines and even the government for allowing the sale of pornographic material. There are many feminists who oppose this view and believe that censoring pornography could lead to other curtailments of free speech.

At the end of this century there remains a question mark over whether pornography corrupts. Is it reasonable to object to the way in which women are portrayed? Are we too liberal in allowing almost anything to be published? Or does the censorship of sexually explicit material erode the right of free speech?

OPINION

'There is no evidence that 'exposure to or use of explicit sexual material plays a significant role in the causation of social or individual harms, such as crime, delinquency, sexual or nonsexual deviancy or severe emotional disturbances.'
A finding of the Obscenity Commission set up by US President Johnson, 1968.

CENSORSHIP TODAY

The reasons given for censorship have altered very little over the twentieth century, but advances in technology and the changing values of society have led to vastly different methods and limits. There are still dictatorships in Africa, Asia and the Middle East where much information is suppressed. In Syria and Iraq the list of banned books is longer than the list of those permitted. Some 10,000 books are banned in Israel. In North Korea political opinion is censored: imported radios have their dials fixed to prevent the reception of foreign programs.

Every year over a hundred journalists are killed throughout the world. Some may be accidentally shot in war zones, but many are assassinated because of their writings. The Irish crime reporter, Veronica Guerlain, was shot because she exposed drugs rings in Dublin, Ireland. Post-Communist Russia now has censorship by the gun: the Russian 'Mafia' has killed many journalists who have not heeded its warnings. In the 1990s there have been numerous massacres in Algeria: many local and foreign journalists have been killed for asking too many questions and printing information that their murderers want suppressed.

OPPOSING CENSORSHIP

Article 19 is a group founded in 1986 to oppose censorship. It takes its name from Article 19 of the United Nations Declaration of Human Rights, which guarantees freedom of expression. The UN Declaration of Human Rights was formulated in 1948, but unfortunately many of the countries that signed up for it have not abided by it. In 1991 Article 19 surveyed seventy-seven countries. In sixty-two of them people were detained for peacefully expressing their opinions. In twenty-seven countries people, including journalists, were tortured, killed or otherwise maltreated on account of their opinions. These countries included China, Indonesia, Turkey, Somalia and Ethiopia.

The United States has a long history of banning books from school libraries. Banned authors have included Charles Dickens, Mark Twain, John Steinbeck and Judy Blume. In the 1990s the National Association of Christian Educators and Citizens for Excellence in Education helped to elect 450 fundamentalist Christians onto school boards. From this position of authority they can affect the curriculum and reading. Hundreds of school districts have had their elementary school reading challenged.

A demonstration against censorship in the USA in 1990.

THE INTERNET

Technological advances have raised new concerns about censorship. Some people argue that the Internet is vast and anarchic, and so it must remain. But others maintain that vast profits are being made by Internet providers who should take some responsibility for the information they carry. In the United States some 200 children have been abused by paedophiles who have arranged meetings through the use of Internet chat lines. There is also hardcore child pornography on the Internet that is illegal in all the countries it reaches. The European Union is drawing up guidelines for the Internet, and the German government has indicated that it is willing to prosecute. Many people fear that once any form of censorship is imposed on the Internet, there will be political censorship too.

Internet users in a cyber-cafe. The Internet poses a serious challenge to those who want to censor its contents.

In the United States there are moves towards filtering the Internet to ensure that certain web sites cannot be accessed. Filters are to be used by libraries, cyber-cafes and work-places. Some US senators are demanding that funding be cut to schools and libraries if they do not use a filter. The American Library Association says that any filtering is censorship. The Electronic Privacy Information Centre showed that one filter found only fifteen suitable sites when searching for information about the National Association for the Advancement of Colored People. There were 4,000 sites available. Another filter blocked feminist and atheist discussion groups, HIV resources pages, the animal rights resource site, and criticism of itself.

TO CENSOR, OR NOT TO CENSOR?

The fight against censorship has often taken place on the international stage. Index on Censorship is an organization that lists instances of censorship throughout the world and publishes banned writing in its quarterly journal. This organization tries to expose instances of censorship whenever they occur.

So is there any evidence to suggest that in some situations censorship can be justified? Should there be some regulation of information, not least to protect the more vulnerable members of our society? If so, who appoints the regulator? And how can we be sure that the regulator will represent our interests? What is morally reprehensible to one person is another's freedom of expression. There is no doubt that censorship will continue in the twenty-first century; but it is unlikely that there will ever be agreement on when and where it is acceptable.

Is it all right for young people to watch violent films, such as Rambo *and* The Terminator? *Or should some censorship be imposed on films and on people's viewing habits?*

GLOSSARY

Abdicate to give up responsibilities and rights or, in the case of a monarch, to renounce the throne.

Annex to take over something, e.g. a country.

Blacklist a list of people or organizations under suspicion of doing something wrong.

Blasphemy behaviour that shows disrespect for God.

Communism a political system based, in theory, on the equal distribution of wealth among all people.

Consensus general or widespread agreement between people.

Coup an abbreviation of *coup d'état* – the sudden seizure of government by unelected people, usually the military.

Democracy a political system in which the government consists of representatives elected by the people.

Dissent disagreement.

Draft dodgers people who evade the draft (the American term for compulsory military service).

Fascism a political theory based on a strong central government with suppression of all opposition and criticism.

Feminism a movement that supports equal rights for women.

Fundamentalism a belief in the literal truth of a religion, e.g. Christian fundamentalists believe that everything in the Bible is true.

Infanticide the killing of babies and young children.

Liberal a person who is tolerant of different points of view and has social and political opinions that favour progress and reform.

Monopoly the exclusive control of something, e.g. a product or service.

Obscenity an indecent act.

Orthodoxy the holding of established or accepted opinions.

Paedophile an adult intent on having sex with children.

Propaganda the organized spread of opinions or beliefs to assist the cause of (usually) a government.

Proprietor an owner.

Radical favouring extreme changes in social, political or economic conditions.

Ratify to approve formally, usually by the signing of a document.

Recant to withdraw a former belief or statement.

Subversive liable to undermine or overthrow a government.

Terrorism the use of armed action and violence to achieve a political aim.

Unexpurgated a book, film etc. with potentially obscene or offensive sections left in.

BOOKS TO READ

Amnesty International annual report
This report documents human rights abuses, including restrictions on free speech.

Attacks on Freedom of the Press by Reporters Sans Frontieres
An annual survey by journalists.

Censorship by Christian Wolmar, Wayland, 1990
A round-up of the issues around censorship.

Censorship in Schools by Victoria Sherrow, Enslow, 1996
A discussion of issues surrounding various types of censorship occurring in schools; including literature, courses and text books.

Defending Pornography by Nadine Strossen, Scribener, New York, 1996
The President of the American Civil Liberties Union argues that state control of obscene publications does not help women.

Encyclopaedia of Censorship by Derek Jones (editor), Fitzroy Dearborne, 1999
Different types and examples of censorship.

Fighting Words by Kent Greenwalt, Princeton University Press, 1996
Analysis of First Amendment cases.

The First Amendment: Freedom of Speech, Religion and the Press by Leah Farish, Enslow, 1998
A young adults' guide to the arguments.

Free Speech: From Newspapers to Music Lyrics by Karen Zeinart, Enslow, 1995
Charts the development of free speech in the United States.

Index on Censorship
A bi-monthly round-up of censored global news, published by a non-profit-making company, Writers & Scholars International Ltd.

The Project Censored Yearbook
An annual round-up of censored US news stories.

USEFUL ADDRESSES

UK

Amnesty International
99-119 Rosebery Avenue
London EC1R 4RE

Article 19
Lancaster House
33 Islington High Street
London N1 9LH

Index on Censorship
Lancaster House
33 Islington High Street
London N1 9LH

Liberty
21 Tabard Street
London SE1

USA

American Booksellers' Association
560 White Plains Road
Tarrytown, New York 10591

**American Booksellers' Foundation
for Free Expression**
560 White Plains Road
Tarrytown, New York 10591

American Civil Liberties Union
National Headquarters
132 West 43rd Street
New York 10036

American Library Association
Office for Intellectual Freedom
50 East Huron Street
Chicago, Illinois 60611

American Society of Journalists and Authors
1501 Broadway
Suite 302
New York 10036

Freedom to Write Committee
PEN American Center
568 Broadway
New York 10012

INDEX

Numbers in **bold** refer to illustrations.